Lakeland

by

William Rollinson, M.A., Ph.D., F.R.G.S.

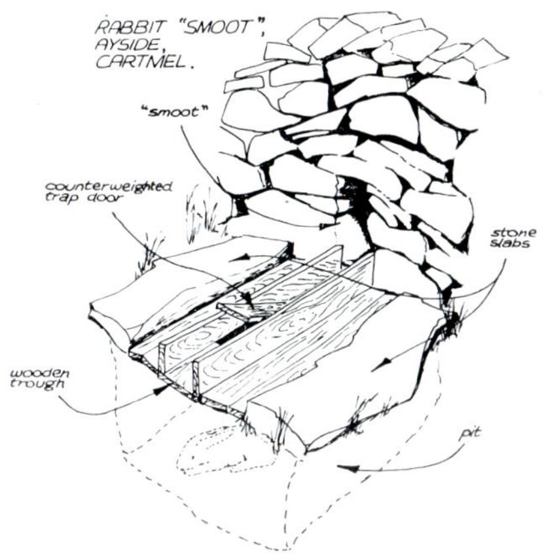

DALESMAN BOOKS
1975

30p.

THE DALESMAN PUBLISHING COMPANY LTD.
CLAPHAM (via Lancaster), NORTH YORKSHIRE.

First Published 1969
Second edition 1972
Third edition 1975

ISBN: O 85206 313 X

Acknowledgements.

I wish to thank the staff of the Cumbrian Record Offices at Kendal and Carlisle, the Leconfield Estate Company Ltd., Mr. B. L. Thompson of Troutbeck, Mr. R. Stewardson and Mr. A. Frearson of Cartmel for valuable assistance in the compilation of this monograph. I am also indebted to Mrs. Betty Thomson for typing the manuscript, to Miss Joan Treasure for the maps, and to Mr. David Kirk for the line drawings.

W. R.

Printed in Great Britain by
GEORGE TODD & SON,
Marlborough Street, Whitehaven.

An Introduction

ONE of the most characteristic and familiar features of the Lakeland landscape is the network of dry-stone walls which divide the fells into an intricate and web-like pattern. Few tourists visiting the area for the first time can have failed to marvel at these stone fences traversing steep slopes, surmounting rocky outcrops, and clinging to the fellsides as if they had not been built but rather had grown out of the mountain side like the rowan and the blaeberries. Few walkers can have failed to appeciate the welcome shelter of a stout stone wall on a wet and windy mountain side, and few fell wanderers on Great Gable can have ceased to admire the beauty of the stone mosaic casting long shadows on the sunlit fields of Wasdale Head far below.

So familiar have the walls become that it is indeed difficult to imagine the Lakeland scene without them and yet, in spite of their ancient appearance, they are a relatively recent addition to the cultural landscape; most of them date from the period between the middle of the 18th century to the middle of the 19th. Until that time most of the Cumbrian fells remained unenclosed; even in 1769 the northern part of Westmorland was described as "open Champaign country"[1] and in 1794 the famous absentee Bishop of Llandaff and gentleman farmer, Richard Watson, estimated that three quarters of Westmorland was waste or common land.[2] Within a hundred years, however, the hedges and stone walls of the fells had ceased to be unusual features; instead they had become an accepted part of the landscape, as much part of Cumbria as the mountains, lakes, and tarns themselves.

It would be wrong to regard the stone walls of Lakeland merely as boundaries between pastures for they are more than this. Sheep farmers have long appreciated the shelter which a solidly-built stone wall affords a hillside flock in inclement weather. This protection cannot be provided by 20th century barbed wire fences. Similarly, short lengths of stone wall were constructed in order to stop sheep from straying over precipices or into gullies. Over a hundred years ago the shepherds of Ennerdale kept in repair a wall which prevented their sheep from wandering onto the front of Pillar Rock,[3] and similar walls, though now decayed, may be seen on the summit of Dow Crags in the Coniston range.

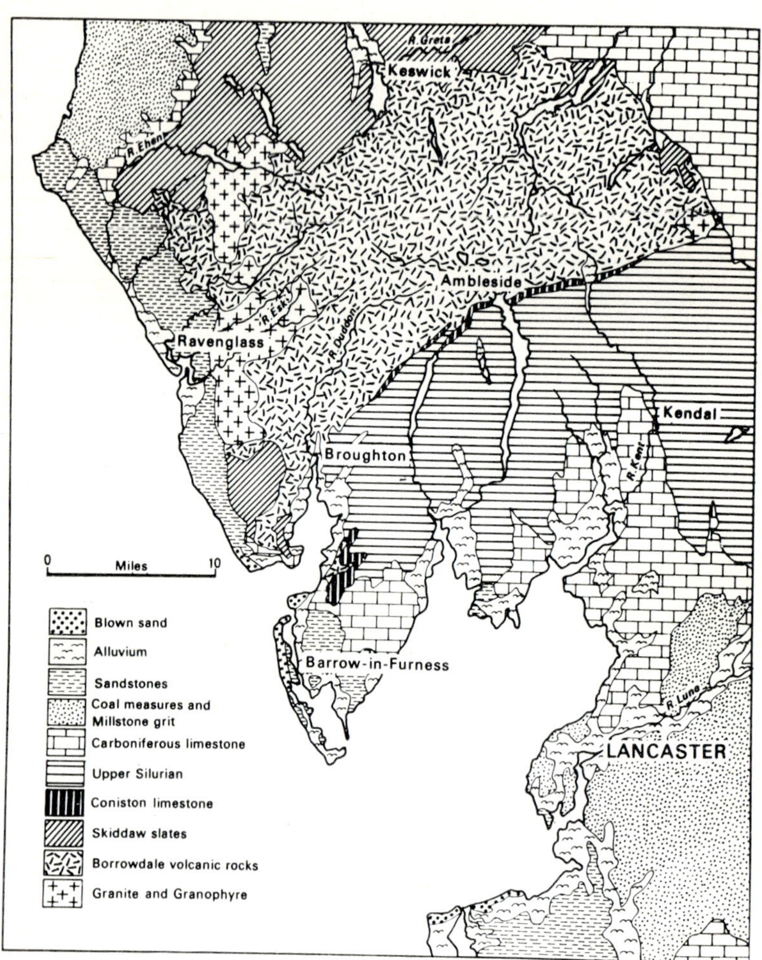

FIG. 2.—A GEOLOGICAL MAP

OF THE LAKE DISTRICT

AN INTRODUCTION

As well as enclosing areas of rough pasture and preventing sheep from becoming crag-fast, stone walls and fences were built specifically to channel sheep from the high fells down to the farmstead for lambing and shearing. Such "out-gangs" take the form of a wide-mouthed funnel narrowing down to a green trackway bounded by parallel dry-stone walls culminating in sheep pens. A particularly fine 18th or 19th century example may be seen in Scandale, north of Ambleside. Free access to the fells was, of course, particularly important in the days before the enclosure movement when the fellsides were common and the rights of "sheep-gates" were jealously guarded. In 1681, at Seathwaite in Dunnerdale, there appears to have been "strife and variance" concerning a "sheep-gate" and a jury was set up to give a judgement.[4] It recommended the construction of "rayles" by which the sheep might be driven from the fields to the fell tops, to be built "at or before the 24th day of June upon payne of 6s. 8d. every one making default." Although the form of these "rayles" is not described, they may have been wooden rather than stone fences.

Lakeland walls, then, serve a variety of functions; they also show a remarkable diversity of styles and rock types which can vary from one part of the area to another. It is the aim of this booklet to examine not only the age and purpose of the stone fences but also to study their variety from region to region and to determine their characteristic features. The building of these walls marks an important yet neglected phase in the history of the landscape of the Lake District.

References

1. Russel, P., and Price, O., (eds.), *England Displayed,* 1769, Volume 1, p. 237.

2. Pringle, A., *A General View of the Agriculture of the County of Westmorland,* 1794 (with an introduction by Richard Watson, Bishop of Llandaff), pp. 6-7.

3. Palmer, W. T., *Odd Corners in English Lakeland,* 1937, p. 74.

4. Collingwood, W. G., "An Award concerning Sheep-gates, Seathwaite, Dunnerdale, 1681," *Trans. Cumberland and Westmorland Antiquarian and Archaeological Society, New Series,* Volume 8, 1908, pp. 352-354.

1. Some General Characteristics

ALTHOUGH it has already been suggested that there are regional differences in walling styles within Lakeland there are, nevertheless, certain common characteristics which ought to be appreciated at the outset. The most obvious is the absence of any form of mortar, cement, or binding material, for the dry-stone fences rely for their stability only on the skill of the wallers. The 18th and 19th century walls are, as Dr. Arthur Raistrick points out,[1] structures in equilibrium in which the principal load is carried down through each skilfully laid stone course on to the foundation below. To the untutored eye many of the Cumbrian stone walls appear to be merely haphazardly arranged stones piled on top of one another, but nothing could be further from the truth and more than one amateur suburban gardener has seen the errors of this misconception when his newly built dry-stone wall collapsed after the first winter frost.

To construct a dry-stone wall which would stand for centuries and be proof against the elements, the wily attention of sure-footed Herdwick sheep and the clamberings of fell-walkers, it was first necessary to set the wall on a good footing. Once the line of the wall had been established, a shallow trench was prepared some four or five feet wide, and on a firm sub-soil or a bed-rock foundation the footing stones were located in place. These large and usually square-shaped boulders were set in two parallel rows with the squared ends facing outwards (Fig. 3); often these were the largest stones to be incorporated in the walls and frequently they came from field clearances. The largest footing stones known to the author occur near Far Kiln Bank in the Duddon valley (G.R. 214936)* where the size of the stones — often many feet across — is reminiscent of the so-called "cyclopean" architecture of North Wales (Plate 3).

The space between the two rows of footing stones was filled with "hearting," small, irregular rock fragments. This form of filling was preferred because irregular fragments bind together firmly under pressure. Such was the founda-

---

*Grid references refer to the One-Inch Ordnance Survey map, Tourist edition.

Plate 1. Contrasting patterns in Wasdale. The small, irregular fields on the valley floor, some containing clearance cairns formed from surplus stones, contrast markedly with the more regular "intakes" of a later period which stretch up the fellside.

tion on which the wall depended for its stability and well-being. The second "course," or layer of stones, was then laid, care being taken to see that each stone rested on two stones in the course below. The care with which stones were located was an integral part of the art of walling and a true craftsman, having once picked up a stone, would not put it down again until it had been finally positioned in the wall.

The second and subsequent courses were generally built as two faces, the gap between the two being skilfully packed with hearting stones. After several courses had been constructed the "through" stones were laid at intervals. These "throughs" are, as the name suggests, larger stones running across the wall and often projecting out from it on both sides; their main function is to tie the two faces together and to prevent the wall from "bellying out" (Fig. 3). A well-built wall often had two or more sets of throughs at different heights above the footing stones. So important were the throughs considered to be that many walling contracts specified the number of through courses in each wall as well as the spacing of each set of throughs in the course (see page 26).

As the wall increased in height, so the width at the top decreased to perhaps one or two feet. This was achieved by using smaller stones and setting them into the walls slightly, thereby producing a wall which was thicker at the base than at the top. Many walling agreements state precisely what this wall "batter" should be. In order to attain the correct height and batter, a wooden frame corresponding to the shape of the wall was sometimes used as a guide. When the wall reached the required height it was finished off with a final course of thinner, slab-like stones on top of which the "cams" or coping stones were set. These were frequently slate-like stones roughly the same size, stacked on edge and all leaning in the same way; their main purpose was to discourage sheep from leaping over the wall. The final act in the building of a wall was to insert wedge stones wherever necessary to fill any remaining gaps.

This is a simplified general account of the building of a typical Lakeland dry-stone wall during the 18th or 19th century, yet there are other characteristics which remain to be mentioned. The observant fell walker will have noticed how, on steeply sloping ground, the stones in a wall remain horizontal irrespective of the angle of slope. Nowhere is this better seen than in that splendid wall — one of the finest in Lakeland — which snakes its way over Low Pike on the Fairfield range. Just south of Low Pike the wall ascends an almost vertical outcrop of rock (G.R. 374077) and here, as elsewhere in the wall, the long axes of the stones remain horizontal (Plate 5). A lesser-known characteristic, but one which is of some importance, concerns the angle at which the stones in a well-constructed wall were laid; wherever possible the stones slope outwards so that rain-water drains off the wall rather than running inward and soaking the hearting. In this way the centre of the wall remains dry at all times of the year and the risk of damage by frost expansion in winter is reduced. If for any reason the hearting of a wall is attacked by frost, whole sections of wall can deteriorate rapidly.

Wall "heads" are common in those walls built during the enclosure period of the 18th and 19th centuries; such features generally mark the boundary of lengths of walls belonging to different people. If, for example, under an enclosure award (see chapter 3) a landowner was required to build one section of a common wall, his neighbour might be required to complete the wall and the junction between the two lengths would be clearly marked by a "head", indicating the sections for which the landowners had responsibility for upkeep and repair. A "head" was con-

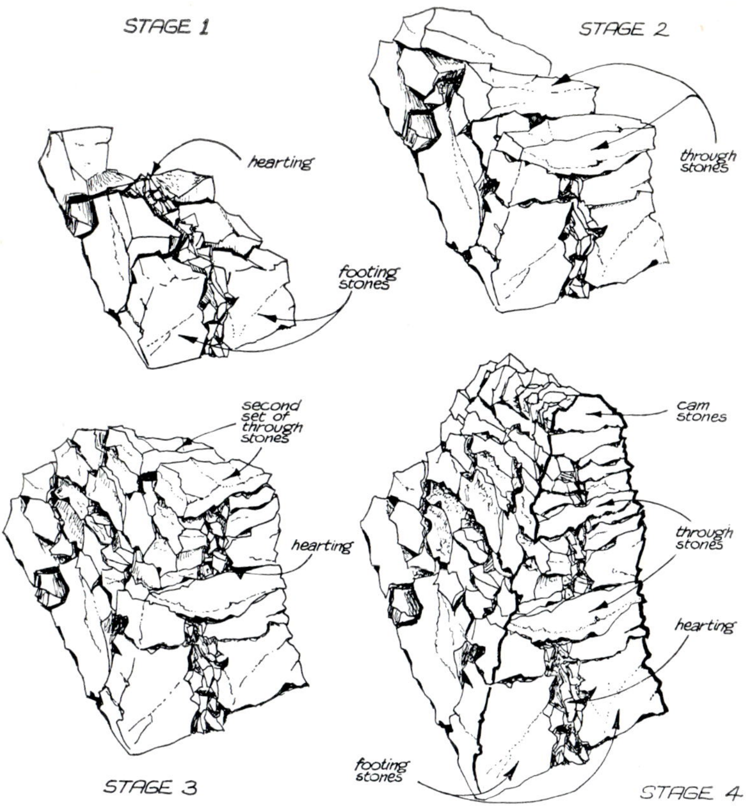

Fig. 3. STAGES IN THE CONSTRUCTION OF A DRY-STONE WALL

structed by building into the wall a number of large stones, one on top of the other, so that the square corners form a vertical, clear-cut join in the wall (Plate 6).

Perhaps even more conspicuous than wall "heads" are "hogg-holes," square holes left in the base of many Lakeland walls. A "hogg" is a yearling sheep and these openings in the stone fences allowed sheep to pass unhindered from one part of the "heaf," or pasture, to another. Usually square in shape, measuring less than two feet by two, these "hogg-holes" could be opened or closed when necessary merely by rolling a stone slab or boulder across the opening

(Plate 4). In most cases "hogg-holes" are constructed by roofing over a gap left in the lower courses of a wall with a large slab capable of supporting the remaining upper courses, but variations on this theme may be observed, for example, in the Lickle valley where one or two unusual instances of gable-shaped holes may be seen. Occasionally small holes or rabbit "smoots" were left in the base of walls to allow unsuspecting rabbits through the walls to a slyly concealed trap (see title page).

Having investigated some of the general characteristics of 18th and 19th century walls, we can consider some of the varieties of walling which exist within the area. Variation in size, height, width and style largely depends on the material available for the building of the wall, and this in turn depends on the geology of the region. The complexity of Lake District geology is well known and much has been written about it.[2] An aspect which has not received much attention is the manner in which building materials closely reflect the solid geology. This is particularly true of the pre-19th century period when, because of transport difficulties, building stone was carted only the minimum distance overland. One has only to recall the silver-grey limestone farms of the Carboniferous Limestone areas of West Cumbria and Low Furness, the warm mottled-pink granite of the Eskdale cottages, the rust-red sandstone buildings of St. Bees and the Eden valley, the dark slate farms of the northern fells around Skiddaw, or the sea-green slate buildings of the Tilberthwaite area, to appreciate this. The same is true of the dry-stone walls.

Broadly speaking, the Lake District may be considered as a dome or core of ancient, resistant rocks forming the high fells, surrounded by a discontinuous ring of younger, less resistant rocks such as the Carboniferous Limestones, Coal Measures, and sandstones of the Cumbrian foothills. In several areas erosion has exposed complex crystalline intrusions such as the Eskdale and Shap granites, the Ennerdale granophyres, and the igneous rocks of Carrock Fell. Each of these geological formations has produced changes in the pattern and texture of wall building which is clearly discernible to the practised eye.

The oldest rocks in Lakeland are the Skiddaw Slates, a collective name for a series of dark-coloured slates, shales, and grits. As their name suggests, they are found in the northern part of the Cumbrian dome in the Skiddaw-Blencathra area, though there is a smaller area in south-west Cumbria outcropping to form the Black Combe range. The

Plate 2. Walling in limestone near Arnside, Cumbria.

Skiddaw Slates were probably formed as sands and muds in a shallow sea some 450 million years ago, but under the long-continuing action of earth pressures and mountain building movements they were converted into the slates and shales which are so characteristic of the area.

One of the features which distinguishes this series of rocks from those of the central group of fells is the well-marked cleavage, and a tendency to split into slabs along cleavage and bedding plains. This, in turn, has meant that although there are exceptions such as the precipitous roof-ridge of Sharp Edge on Blencathra, on the whole the profiles of mountains composed of the Skiddaw Slate series tend to be smooth and rounded in outline, typified by Skiddaw and Blencathra in the north and in the south by Black Combe, aptly described by the Cumbrian poet, Norman Nicholson, as "a gum-boil of a mountain." Within this series termed the Skiddaw Slates there are a number of sub-divisions — the Loweswater Flags, the Mosser Slates, the Kirkstile Slates — these are just a few, but all tend to exhibit a fissile quality and dry-stone walls built in this material are usually distinctive.

The central fells of the Lake District are composed of the Borrowdale Volcanic rocks, a great thickness of fine volcanic ashes, coarse breccias or agglomerates, lavas, and muds poured out and deposited during a long period of volcanic activity some 400 million years ago. Clearly, the Borrowdale Volcanic series includes a great variety of rock types ranging from the green slates of Coniston and Tilberthwaite to the massive Langdale rhyolites. On the whole these rocks are relatively resistant to erosion, producing a much more rugged, wild landscape than the Skiddaw Slates in the north. Within the Borrowdale Volcanic series are most of the impressive mountain ranges — Great Gable, Scafell and Scafell Pike, Helvellyn, the Langdale Pikes, Coniston Old Man — names to quicken the pulse of any rock climber for if the major rock climbs are plotted on a geology map, most of them occur within this central volcanic belt.

Walls within this Borrowdale Volcanic region tend to be massively built (Plate 4). Within this area, however, there are some interesting and unique features. In one or two places volcanic activity has resulted in the formation of columnar hexagonal columns similar to the Giant's Causeway basalts of Antrim, Northern Ireland, though on a smaller scale; examples may be seen on the summit of Dow

Crags in the Coniston range, Mardale Ill Bell, and in Torver Beck, a hundred or so yards downstream from the bridge which carries the Walna Scar road across the stream. There are similar examples in the Lickle Valley, west of Stephenson Ground Crag.[3] At Stephenson Ground Farm (G.R. 235932) some of these hexagonal pillars have been incorporated into the walls in a most practical and ingenious manner. Plate 7 illustrates the way in which these unusual rhyolitic columns have been used to bridge a small stream, allowing the beck to flow through a gap in the wall yet preventing animals from straying from one side of the wall to the other.

South of the central area of the Borrowdale Volcanic rocks is the third of the major geological systems, the Silurian Slates, shales and flags, a series of younger rocks probably deposited in a shallow sea some 350 million years ago; they now form the lower, more subdued landscape of southern Lakeland. Here there are no major peaks and no sheer rock faces but rather the rounded, wooded hills of the Furness Fells between Coniston lake and Windermere. The dry-stone walls in this area are more akin to those in the Skiddaw Slate region for the Silurian rocks generally have a well-marked cleavage plain and the rock is fissile. In areas where the Coniston and Brathay Flags occur, notably in Coniston, Hawkshead and Ambleside, stone fences composed of vertical "flags" or slates may be seen. They are not wired together as in North Wales, but interlocked, edge to edge (Plate 8). Frost action and soil creep may result in the fences leaning over in drunken disarray and they require greater upkeep than the more orthodox stone walls.

In addition to the three major rock types already described, a fourth may be distinguished, namely the complex crystalline rocks which were intruded into the earth's crust from deep-seated magmas and which have now been exposed at the surface by the stripping away of the overlying rocks. The two most extensive areas exposed are the Ennerdale granophyres and the Eskdale granites. The construction of the dry-stone walls in these localities differs little from walls in the Borrowdale Volcanic country, but the colour is noteworthy for these walls have quite a distinct pinkish colour. Similarly in the eastern part of the Lake District, near Shap, the granite there shows the same pink colouring.

Many of the 18th and 19th century walls on the high fells were built with stone specially quarried near to the site, but many others, particularly those on or near to the valley floor, were constructed from the smooth, rounded boulders from the beds of streams or from the boulders which had to be cleared from the fields in order to improve the land.

Plate 3 (top left). "Cyclopean" construction in the Duddon valley near Ulpha. These huge boulders are probably a result of field clearances. The folded Ordnance Survey map in the centre of the photograph gives the scale.

Plate 4 (top right). A "hogg-hole," Borrowdale Volcanic rock, Fairfield range.

Plate 5 (bottom left). A well-constructed wall in Borrowdale Volcanic rock below Low Pike on the Fairfield range. The striking way in which stones are set horizontally in spite of the steeply sloping ground is particularly noticeable in this example.

Plate 6 (bottom right). A wall head near Coniston.

Plate 7 (top left). Ingenuity in stone walling; these rhyolitic hexagonal pillars have been used to bridge a small beck at Stephenson Ground farm in the Lickle valley. An exposure of columnar rhyolite in the Borrowdale Volcanic series occurs west of Stephenson Ground Crag.

Plate 8 (top right). A stone fence composed of flags set edge to edge, near Hawkshead. These flags are carefully interlocked.

Plate 9 (bottom left). Ice- or water-worn Eskdale Granite boulders have been used in the construction of this fine wall near Ravenglass. Note that the larger stones have been used in the lower courses.

Plate 10 (bottom right). A wall of great thickness at Wasdale Head. Here the wall is merely a depository for the stones which have been cleared from the small fields on the floor of the valley.

Plate 11. Water-worn sea-shore pebbles form the basic building material for this turf and stone dike on the coast near Bootle, Cumbria.

The rounded glacial rocks and the water-worn stones of the valley bottoms contrast with the rough, angular rocks used in the construction of the fellside walls, a contrast which can be observed in almost any part of Lakeland (Plate 9). In several valleys the stones cleared from the land were more than could be used in the building of the walls and consequently huge piles of stones or "clearance cairns" can be seen in the middle of the fields. This was a feature which did not escape the ever-observant Jonathan Otley; in 1818 he wrote:

Wasdale Head comprises a level area of 400 acres of land divided by stone walls into irregular fields, which have been cleared with great industry and labour; as appears from the enormous heaps of stones, piled up from the surplus after completing the enclosure.[4]

Alternatively, the thickness of the walls was increased considerably in order to utilise the stones; consider for a minute the thickness of the walls in Mickleden, Great Langdale or Wasdale Head where the corners of the fields have been filled up and rounded off in order to dispose of the excess stones (Plate 10). At Bowderdale, near Wasdale Head, the surplus stones have been incorporated into a bastion-like wall many feet thick.

Around the edge of the Cumbrian mountains the silver-grey limestones, the red sandstones and the darker grits of the coal measures all occur. Often they are blanketed with a covering of boulder clay left by the ice sheets and therefore building stone is not as readily available as in the fells. Moreover, on the lower ground of the West Cumbrian coastal plain, the Eden Valley, Furness and Cartmel, where conditions were suitable, it was cheaper and equally effective to plant a quickthorn hedge rather than build a dry-stone wall and consequently hedges abound in these areas. However, near to the coast strong winds and salt spray prevented the growth of all but the most hardy and stunted hedgerows and in these instances a different type of building material was used — sea-shore pebbles.

Although strictly dry-stone walls in the sense that no cement was used, the walls (or rather banks) were formed of layers of rounded pebbles, the interstices being packed with soil. After a year or so they became so completely grassed over that it is often difficult to detect the layers of stones which form the heart of the wall (Plate 11). Examples of such embankments are not difficult to find on the Furness and West Cumbrian seaboard; when the common fields of Walney Island were enclosed at the end of the 18th century and the beginning of the 19th, almost all the field boundaries were built in this way, there being no other serviceable form of building material on the island.

Here, then, we have some of the differences in material and consequently in building styles of our 18th and 19th century walls, differences which add both interest and character to an already varied landscape and which can be appreciated fairly readily with but a minimum of experience.

References for Chapter 1

1. Raistrick, A., *Pennine Walls*, 1966, p. 22.
2. The standard work, now available once again as a reprint, is still Professor J. E. Marr's *Geology of the Lake District*, 1916. A recent addition to the literature is E. H. Shackleton's popular yet authoritative *Lakeland Geology*, while a short but lucid account will be found in Professor F. J. Monkhouse's *The English Lake District*, 1960.
3. Mitchell, G. H., "The Borrowdale Volcanic Series of the Dunnerdale Fells, Lancashire," *Liverpool and Manchester Geological Journal*, Volume 1, 1956, p. 437.
4. Otley, J., *A Concise Description of the English Lakes and adjoining Mountains*, 1818, p. 133.

2. Early Walls and Fences

THE art of building dry-stone walls is undoubtedly an ancient one and Prehistoric Man developed the technique. At Ewe Close, Crosby Ravensworth, one of the best-known Romano-British settlements in northern England, are some of the finest examples of early dry-stone walls in Cumbria, examples not only of hut circles but also of stone-fenced "Celtic" fields. A similar pattern is repeated on the Carboniferous Limestones of Low Furness at Urswick, south of Ulverston, and again at Lanthwaite Green near Crummock Water, at Barnscar on Birkby Fell, at Little Arrow Moor, Coniston, and in several other places.[1] These early stone walls defy accurate dating and we must wait until the medieval period before documentary evidence for the building of walls can be furnished.

One of the earliest fences for which there is documentary proof is the Rydal fence. Although it is not strictly a dry-stone wall it nevertheless deserves a mention here. In 1275 Sir Roger fitz Gilbert de Lancaster acquired "Rydale, Amelseter and Loghrigg," and adjoining this territory were the lands of Troutbeck, Applethwaite and Windermere, owned by William de Lyndesey. Unfortunately, but by no means uncommonly in those days, William's tenants allowed their livestock to stray over into Roger's territory who, in order to prevent a repetition, decided to enclose his manor with a fence. Consequently, in 1277, an agreement was drawn up between Roger de Lancaster, William de Lyndesey, and a third party, Margaret de Ros.[2] Roger undertook to make a fence of 160 perches in length (i.e. almost three-quarters of a mile) from the highest point of the park at Rydal along the common boundary between Rydal and Scandale; similarly, William agreed to build the same length of fencing along the same boundary as far as a place described as "the crag in the green cove," a location which cannot now be identified. Furthermore, Roger agreed to construct another fence between Rydal and Grasmere from Rydal Water along Nab Scar to Lord's Crag, while William agreed to continue it to a point mid-way between Lord's Crag and Erne Crag, and Margaret de Ros undertook to construct the fence as far as Erne Crag. It was agreed that all these fences should be made before Michaelmass, 1277.

A Book of Severall painable Hedges. To be made and upholden by the Tenants of Troutbeck according as they are hereafter set down by their proper Names, and for their respective Tenements, with the quantity of each mans Respective Dale of Hedge or fence as they Lye in Order, Taken the first day of May 1680. By the approbation of the Lords Jury, whose Names are hereunto Subscribed, and the Consent of the rest of the Tenants in Troutbeck aforesaid.

First Between the fforest and Woundale Begining At the fforce

	Yards	feet
Edward Howcroft and Thomas Cookson for the Tenants of the Lowest Hundred	7	
Tenants of the Midle Hundred	11	
Tenants of the Highest Hundred	15	
Myles Birkhead for Hayton Tenement	10	2
Stephen Grisdale for half ffire	5	2
James Longmire of Crag	6	2
Thomas Watson	12	1
Joseph Sharp of Townend	8	1
Ditto	4	

Plate 12. Part of the Troutbeck Painable Fence Book, written originally in 1680. This states the length of fence (i.e. stone wall) to be maintained by each tenant.

The question now arises as to what form the fence took. W. G. Collingwood[3] has argued convincingly that it could not have been a dry-stone wall; his reasoning is based on the fact that the ridges over which the fence runs are remarkably free of loose stone and to quarry or cart building material would have been impracticable, particularly since the fences had to be constructed in the short period between May, when the agreement was drawn up, and the following September. Instead he argues that the so-called "fence" was probably made by digging a ditch, throwing up the upcast to form an embankment on top of which a wattle and post fence was erected. Little now remains of this Rydal fence although part of the dike on Nab Scar may still be traced.

Perhaps one of the most fascinating walls in Lakeland is that built by the Cistercian monks of Furness Abbey in the remote and marshy head of the Esk valley. The Cistercians, of course, were inveterate agriculturalists and sheep farming in the Cumbrian fells was an important part of their activities. By the middle of the 13th century this same monastery owned three great tracts of land in the fells — a large part of Borrowdale, the area between Coniston Water and Windermere and about 14,000 acres of sheep pasture in upper Eskdale.[4] Some time between 1284 and 1290 John de Hudleston, Lord of Millom, granted to Furness Abbey the right to enclose the pastures of "Botherhulkil" (Brotherilkeld and "Lincoue" (Lincove) adjoining the forest of Egremont[5]

. . . with a dyke, wall or paling as the abbot and monks should think most convenient for them; but such, nevertheless as harts and does and their fawns could leap.[6] (footnote).

Clearly, such a wall was designed to prevent sheep from straying into the forest of Egremont but one which would not hinder the free movement of deer and fawns. It seems that the abbot chose to construct a dike, which was probably surmounted by some form of wattle fencing similar to the Rydal fence. It can be readily distinguished in Lincove and, indeed, the modern fell-walker should be thankful for the industry of these 13th century monks for their embankment provides a convenient causeway across an otherwise boggy area.

Such documented examples of early medieval walls are rare, but in the later medieval period they become more common. One of the best documented areas is the town-

---

Footnote " . . . fossato, muro vel palicio prout predicti abbas et monachi sibi judica verint expedire; ita tamen quod cervi et cerve et eorum fetus dictas clausturas possint transilire."

ship of Troutbeck, near Windermere, where the Browne family, yeoman farmers at Townend farm for more than 300 years, kept detailed and careful records of this farming community.[7] From these records it appears that in 1551 the Forest of Troutbeck,[8] which at that time included both Ambleside and Troutbeck, was divided between the two places by a fence which ran along the summit of the Wansfell ridge. Mr. B. L. Thompson[9] has traced this boundary in some detail from Windermere to "high Pick" (Wansfell Pike), thence to "Cragge of baystons" (Baystones) and so on to "nowit garthe," an old enclosure which can no longer be identified. Although the 1551 award does not define it accurately, it seems that the fence climbed up to the crags of Red Screes and then descended sharply to the summit of Kirkstone Pass. According to the agreement, the fences had to be built by the Ambleside and Troutbeck men by 1st May, 1553, each township being responsible for a carefully determined number of roods (one rood is equivalent to seven yards).

Another document from the Browne collection which illuminates the building and repair of 17th century walls is the Troutbeck Painable Fence Book, first written in 1680.[10] This records the fences (i.e. walls) for which the town was responsible and allocates each man's responsibility for a stated section of wall. The "Lords Jury of Troutbeck" saw to it "that every Tenant, and Tenants shall maintain their painable Fences in good repare or else shall be in pain," that is, fined six shillings and eight pence. Several sections of these painable fences still remain; the fence "between the Forest and Woundale" where it ascends to Red Screes may be observed from "the Struggle," the road from Ambleside to Kirkstone Pass. Plate 12 illustrates that part of the Painable Fence Book which records the length and location of the wall which each tenant was expected to maintain in good order.

No doubt throughout the medieval period assarting, or reclaiming land from the waste, continued and many of these newly formed holdings were probably surrounded by a stone wall. We know, for example, that during the reign of Henry VIII, tenants in the Furness Fells were enclosing land from the commons and that these holdings were "to be hedged with dyke or wall." Indeed, the "ancient enclosures" marked on many of the 18th and 19th century enclosure award maps could well date from this period, but without documentary evidence accurate dating is difficult. It has been suggested[11] that older enclosures can be distinguished by the rounded corners, since in the days before accurate surveying it was easier to build a wall without corners. Certainly it seems that the more irregular shaped fields of the "inland" close to the homestead and on the floors of the valleys such as Great Langdale, Wasdale Head and Borrowdale, contrast with the later, more regular "intakes" on the valley sides, most of which were carved out in the late 18th or early 19th century. Without documentary proof, however, it is unwise to assign a date to these walls purely on the basis of the shape of the enclosure.

By the early 18th century, but before the period of the Enclosure Acts, dry-stone walls surounding farms and hamlets must have been common enough, though the vast expanse of hills and fellsides remained unenclosed and open. Within a hundred years, however, the walls had pencilled their thin , grey lines across the green pastures of the high fells, dividing them up into great enclosures, and creating the landscape which we now know.

References for Chapter 2

1. Rollinson, William, *A History of Man in the Lake District,* 1967, p. 25.
2. Collingwood, W. G., "The Medieval Fence of Rydal and other Linear Earthworks," *Trans. Cumberland and Westmorland Antiquarian and Archaeological Society,* New Series, Volume 30, 1930, p. 4.
3. Collingwood, W. G., *loc. cit.*
4. Rollinson, William, *op. cit.,* p. 80.
5. The term "forest" does not necessarily mean woodland; in the sense used here it signified land over which the lord of the manor held hunting rights.
6. Furness Abbey Coucher Book, Chetham Society, 1916, Volume 2, Part 2, pp. 565-566.
7. The Browne manuscripts are now in the care of the Cumbria Record Office, Kendal.
8. See 5 above.
9. A recent publication based on a detailed study of the Browne manuscripts by Mr. Bruce L. Thompson, *The Troutbeck Hundreds and the Common Lands of Troutbeck, Westmorland,* gives a fascinating and scholarly account of the history of the town fields and their boundaries.
10. The Painable Fence Book in the Browne Collection is not the original one for the signatures in the document are all in the same hand, showing that it must be a later copy.
11. Ward, E. M., *Days in Lakeland,* 1929, p. 63.

3. The Enclosure Movement Walls

THE enclosure movement in Cumbria was, on the whole, rather late, for agricultural activity in this remote part of north-west England was somewhat backward. Moreover, until the pacification of the Border, this Cumbrian region was constantly harried by Scottish raids and consequently there evolved here an unusual form of communal agriculture, a type of co-arration which allowed for temporary absence of tenants on military service. The local historian Thomas West[1] has described this method of farming the arable land at this time :

. . . the arable land being mixed (i.e. unenclosed) . . . several tenants united in equipping a plough, the absence of the fourth man was no prejudice to the cultivation of his land, which was committed to the care of three.

Although the development of open arable fields within Lakeland was not extensive, there were common fields at Wasdale Head, Nether Wasdale, Coniston, Threlkeld, Mardale, Wet Sleddale, Great Langdale, and elsewhere.[2] With the Union of the Crowns in 1603 the long and bitter story of border warfare came to an end and a period of relative stability allowed the improvement and enclosure of many of the common Township fields.

It appears that many of these arable fields were enclosed by private agreement rather than by any formal or legal decision; many of the open arable fields of Furness were enclosed in this way. However, the vast majority of enclosures in the fells date from the later part of the 18th century and the first half of the 19th, a period which includes the Napoleonic wars when the price of food was high and therefore there was an incentive to enclose and improve the rough fell pasture. Such enclosures were often laid out by land surveyors and the regular pattern of large fields usually stands out in marked contrast to the irregular patchwork of the earlier enclosure of the arable fields. At the same time, too, the impact of the Agricultural Revolution was becoming apparent; new methods of agriculture, new crops, improved breeds of animals were introduced and associated with these innovations was the enclosure movement.

Not everyone benefited from the enclosures. Thousands of small farmers lost their rights of pasture on the common land and many became mere farm labourers, some, paupers. And while the movement resulted in the improvement of agriculture and the amassing of wealth into the pockets of a few landowners and wealthy farmers it meant, in the words of Dr. Raistrick, "the enslavement of the labouring classes."[3] Yet such unfortunate developments were not immediately apparent in Cumbria and many writers and agriculturists commented enthusiastically on the new enclosures. Among them was James Clarke, the Penrith surveyor, whose description in his *Survey of the Lakes* (1787) is typical of this 18th century attitude :

Cultivation of every kind has also undergone a very great change within a few years; and this change originating partly from the spirit of industry diffused by the taking up and division of a great number of commons, has had a surprising effect on the manner of the people; an effect which a man need not have lived or made observations for any great length of time to be sensible of. Thus, though the harvest-cry, and the rural feasts and customs are still preserved and though a boundary stone is on some occasions still sacred, yet the number of hedges is mightily increased, and consequently the necessity of them in a great measure superseded: and I know not that there can be a more remarkable passage in the history of rural civilization, than the substitution of hedges in the place of the rude metes and boundaries so generally used in former times; and thus rendering the watchers of cattle needless, as well as giving beauty to the country itself. I doubt not that there have been almost always hedges in some places and indeed there are many remaining that bear the marks of great antiquity, but the neatness and beauty of them is a very modern improvement at least in these parts.[4]

There were two main methods by which land could be enclosed, either by private agreement between the landowners involved, or by Act of Parliament. Private acts were expensive but under the General Enclosure Act of 1801 the procedure for enclosing common land was standardised and the enclosure movement accelerated. Most of the stone walls of the Lake District were built by Act of Parliament following the General Act in 1801. Under enclosure legislation, Commissioners were empowered to survey the lands to be enclosed, to extinguish common rights on this land, and to reapportion it among the promoters of the legislation and the holders of rights on the old commons. In addition, in order to pay the Commissioners' fees, surveyors' bills and other incidentals, the

Commissioners were empowered to sell sufficient land to cover these costs, while the expense of building the enclosure walls was borne by the recipient of the award.

Most enclosure awards specify exactly a date when all the walls were to be completed, and also who was responsible for the repair and upkeep of the walls and gates. The following extract from the Wasdale Head award, dated January 30th, 1808, is typical of many such documents:[5]

William Ritson his Heirs and Assigns to make and repair two fifth parts of the whole extent of Fence up to Black Cragg beginning nearest the Inclosures and John Benson his Heirs and Assigns to make and repair the remaining three fifths parts thereof and so in the like Proportion to the Extremity of the Boundary.

Other awards specified more precisely the nature of the wall; an award for Shap in 1813 states that certain parts of the land are to be "ring-fenced with a wall six feet high, thirty-six inches at the bottom, and sixteen inches at the top."[6]

Although the construction of the walls was the responsibility of the farmer, he often hired bands of wallers to build the fences to his specification. The following carefully worded draft agreement for walling part of Kirkby Moor, Kirkby Lonsdale, although not within Lakeland proper, is worth printing in full; this particular agreement is undated but must have been drawn up shortly after 1810 when the enclosure award referred to was signed :

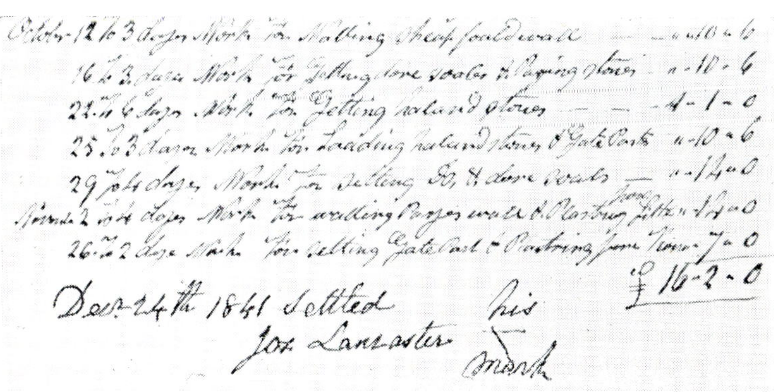

Octobr 12 to 3 days Work for Walling Sheep fold wall — 10 6
16 to 3 days Work for Getting [illegible] stones — 10 6
22 to 6 days Work for Getting [illegible] stones — 4 1 0
25 to 3 days Work for Leading [illegible] stones & Gate Posts — 10 6
29 to 4 days Work for Setting [illegible] — 14 0
Novr 2 to 4 days Work for walling [illegible] — [illegible]
26 to 2 days Work for Setting Gate Post & [illegible] — 7 0
£ 16 2 0

Decr 24th 1841 Settled
Jos Lancaster his mark

Plate 13. A wage receipt relating to work done by Joseph Lancaster, waller, at Lanthwaite Green, in 1841.

Memorandum of an Agreement Between H. B. of Kirkby Lonsdale in the County of Westmorland, Gentleman, and... The Said H. B. being about to inclose an Allotment upon Kirkby Moor in the Said County with a Stone Wall the said.........have proposed and agreed to erect the said Wall hereinafter described. The Said.........agree to get cart and well and substantially to build and finish a Stone Wall on the said Inclosure according to the metes and Bounds described by Edmund Tatham Esquire the Commissioner under the Kirkby Lonsdale Inclosure Act and in manner following that is to say To level the foundation by taking out a Sod along the Line Six Inches deep if required The foundation to be three feet six inches wide at the bottom. To set on three Inches on each side upon the foundation stones and to be carried up gradually to sixteen Inches at the Top The Height of the Wall to be six feet from the higher side of the foundation including the top stones to be set edgewise and not more than six or seven Inches deep The Wall to contain three rows of Throughs in height the first row of which to be laid on the first course of stones above the setting on and the other two rows of throughs to be at equal distance and not laid near the top stones than one foot and the Wall to contain nine Throughs in each row in every rood The Wall to be finished on or before the..............day of..............in the year one thousand eight hundred and...........to the satisfaction of the said H. B. or whom he may appoint In Consideration of which the said H. B. agrees to pay the said........... at and after the rate of..............a rood for each rood or seven yards in length of the said Wall and to advance the same to the said..............at and after the rate of payment for forty roods whenever fifty roods of the said Wall shall from time to time be finished. As witness the hands of the said parties the..............day of..............in the Year of our Lord one thousand eight hundred and..............[7]

It will be appreciated that great skill was involved in the construction of a wall, not merely in the physical building but also in the choice of through stones and top stones. These were sometimes carted considerable distances and their collection involved much labour. The following extracts from a 19th century walling account[8] for work at Lanthwaite, near Crummock Water, illustrate this point :

1837 January 6 To 1 Daye work for Getting threwstone...... at 3/3 per day......3/3
1837 April 10 To 3 Dayes Work for Getting top stones and undersetting at 3/3 per day.........9/9
1841 August 5 To 4 dayes Work for Getting settle stones and top stones.........14/0

Plate 14. A very fissile rock has been used in the construction of this wall at the side of the Garburn Road, Troutbeck, Windermere. The stone probably came from an old quarry nearby. The marked tendency to split into thin slabs makes this an unsatisfactory building material.

For general walling purposes loose stone from the hillside was used, supplemented with material taken from small quarries specially opened for the purpose. Stone was often carried to the site not on carts, which would have overturned on the steep slopes, but on wooden sleds and many walling accounts refer to "the sledging of stones." Occasionally enclosure awards specify the right to take stones for walling from any part of the area to be enclosed. The Wasdale Head Award, 1808, contains this paragraph :

Any of the Parties to the above award their or any of their Heirs or Assigns are to be at Liberty to get Stones for the making of their respective Fences in their respective Allotments from and out of any part or parts of the Grounds hereby intended to be divided without making any compensation for the same.

No doubt the waller's life was a hard one; often he "bivouaced" on the fellside for weeks on end, walling from sunrise to sunset, coming down to the valley floor only at weekends. He was generally paid by the "rood" of seven yards. Andrew Pringle in 1794 gives us an interesting insight into wage rates :

Masons in summer have from 2s 2d to 2s 6d a day, or 1s 2d or 1st 6d and victuals; and in winter 4d or 6d less. At Millthrope a few are hired all the year at 1s 10d a day wet or dry. When they do their work by the piece, and furnish everything, they are paid 2s or 2s 6d a square yard for a wall of two feet in thickness built with lime; if materials are furnished to their hand, they are paid 8d or 10d a yard. Seven yards and a half in length of a dry stone wall five and a half in height costs 1s 6d or 1s 8d in building.[9]

By 1877, however, the rate for the job had increased to six shillings and six pence per rood.[10] Harsh weather conditions slowed down progress on the walls and in winter snow and ice brought a standstill. The following letter written in 1838 by a land surveyor, Richard Atkinson, to John Marshall, Esq., of Penrith, reports on the progress made in the building of walls on the latter's estates :[11]

The Wallers neglected to get stones to the wall against the Common at Potter Gill before the frost set in, after that they could not make a Road to the stones till after the frost which was followed by wet weather so the wall is not done but the foundation is made and ready to begin in the Autumn when they promise to complete it before Winter.

Such were the difficulties of building the walls in our fell country.

Of individual wallers we know little. Their skill helped to transform the Cumbrian landscape but there is scant evidence of the men themselves. Who, for example, built the splendid wall at an altitude of approximately 1,500 to 2,000 feet between Iron Crag, above Ennerdale, and Scoat Fell? And who was Willie Goodwaller after whom the bridge in Far Easedale was named? However, the waller's skill was certainly recognised; the committee entrusted with the building of Flookburgh Chapel, Cartmel, in 1773, being dissatisfied with the contractor's work, consulted two wallers, William Holm of Kendal and William Mount of Ulverston, and on their expert advice parts of the chapel walls which had already been built were demolished and reconstructed.[12]

By the end of the 19th century the transformation of the fells was complete; the hillsides had been confined and bounded within a network of stone built by craftsmen. Like Joseph Lancaster, who was unable to write his name